FROM SEA TO SHORE
BUCK ISLAND REEF NATIONAL MONUMENT
ST. CROIX

ISBN 978-1-4951-7142-0
Printed in the United States of America by Parrot Press Inc, Fort Wayne, Indiana
First Edition: September 2015

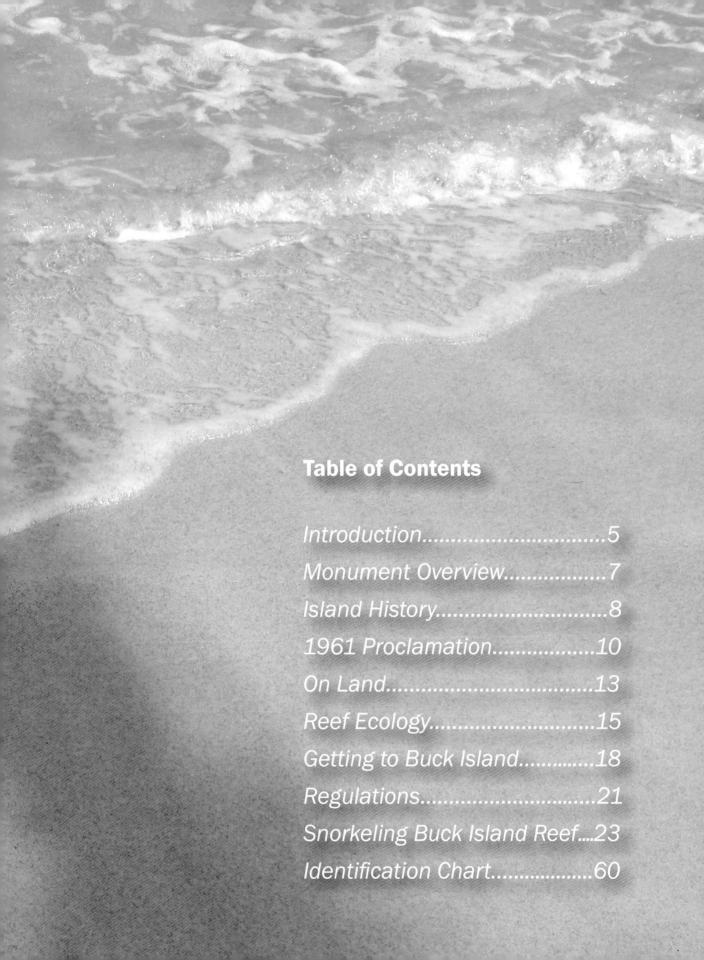

Table of Contents

Introduction.................................5

Monument Overview.................7

Island History............................8

1961 Proclamation.................10

On Land....................................13

Reef Ecology...........................15

Getting to Buck Island.............18

Regulations..............................21

Snorkeling Buck Island Reef....23

Identification Chart..................60

INTRODUCTION

It has been said that if you have never snorkeled before, you have only seen half of what God created. We believe this to be true! And the visual experience of swimming among hundreds of neon blue tangs, multicolored corals, and dancing sea fans can not be adequately described by words. You must see it all with your own eyes.

My first snorkeling experience - ever anywhere – was a decade ago at Buck Island Reef National Monument. I will never forget the first few seconds of that experience as I plunged into the aqua blue water and opened my eyes to see the other half of God's creation. The ever changing light filtering through the water illuminating the shapes, textures, and colors of the abundant life below the water's surface touched me in a way that was stimulating, breathtaking, and profound.

And yet, touring Buck Island is so much more than all that. It is the total experience - - of the boat ride out to the island, the incredible view of St Croix along the way, seeing more shades of blue water than you could ever imagine, and sharing the journey with people on the boat from all over the world - - that combine to make it so special.

While hurricane damage, coral bleaching, and rising ocean temperatures have taken a toll on Buck Island's reef, we have noticed over the past decade that the coral and color are beginning to return here. We salute the men and women of the National Park Service, the Fish and Wildlife Service, and NOAA for their efforts in helping make this happen.

It is important that you know that all the underwater photographs that appear in our book were taken by us in the areas where Buck Island concessionaires take you to snorkel. Specifically, these areas are 1) right off Turtle Beach, 2) along the lagoon snorkeling trail, and 3) the area immediately outside of the trail along the southeastern part of the reef. We have indicated these areas on our map on page 7. The majority of our photographs were taken in 2015 and show underwater terrain and sea life that you will have a good chance of seeing on your tour.

Finally, if you would like to be exposed to more of the under water beauty that you can experience while snorkeling the beaches of the US Virgin Islands, please check out our book "The US Virgin Islands Snorkeling Guide" which is available on Amazon and in local book and gift stores on the islands. And if you have any questions about the material we cover here, please e-mail us at *snorkelingmyway@aol.com*. We would love to continue the conversation.

Enjoy Buck Island!

— Jim and Sarah

BUCK ISLAND REEF NATIONAL MONUMENT OVERVIEW

Buck Island Reef National Monument is located a mile and a half off St. Croix's northeastern shore. The Monument consists of a little over 19,000 acres, which includes the 176 acre uninhabited island and 18,839 acres of underwater terrain and coral reef.

The unique beauty of Buck Island is hardly a well-kept secret. National Geographic Magazine voted Turtle Beach on Buck as one of the world's most beautiful beaches. Travelocity™ selected Buck Island as one of the top ten most eco-friendly places in the world to visit. And CNN© has ranked the Monument as one of the top ten best places to snorkel in the United States. In fact, Buck's snorkeling trail is one of only three snorkeling trails in the US.

While most people come to Buck Island to snorkel, there are a variety of other activities you can do on the Monument. There is a designated scuba diving area located not far from the underwater snorkeling trail. It has a few moorings available for boats. Diedrichs Point and Turtle Beach have grills, picnic tables, and toilets and are available for picnics and family gatherings.

The island also has a moderately difficult hiking trail that takes about 45 minutes to complete. It leads you to a fabulous observation point where you get a bird's eye view of the island, and when the conditions are clear and favorable you can see St. Thomas and St. John. If you elect to hike this trail, be certain to wear comfortable shoes and take drinking water with you. The hike is somewhat rocky, steep in areas, and always a bit on the warm side.

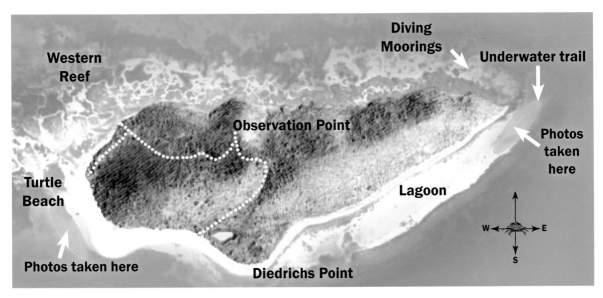

BUCK ISLAND.....

For over 2000 years, Buck Island has been visited by ancient hunters seeking conch, turtle eggs, and fish.

1667

Francois Blondel is credited with making the first map of Buck Island.

600

Archeological digs have unearthed cooking sites and pottery that reflect the aesthetics of the Ostionoid people of this period.

1789

A signal station is built on Buck Island's highest point by the Danish government.

1000

Buck Island continues to be visited by native fishermen interested in harvesting conch. Archaeologists have unearthed many conch shells on the island that have holes in them, indicating that they were harvested by humans.

1754

The first settlement house is built on Buck Island by Johann Diedrich, Christiansted Town Clerk.

1797

The slave ship Mary sinks near Buck Island. The crew and 240 slaves were rescued and brought to safety in Christiansted.

...SANDS OF TIME

1800
Buck Island is clear cut for Lignum Vitae tree lumber to be used for ship building. This makes the island a pasture land for large herds of goats.

1900
Vegetation on the island is repeatedly burned to create pasture land for goats.

1961
President Kennedy issues Presidential Proclamation 3443 that establishes the Buck Island Reef National Monument.

The Proclamation mandates that the area be managed by the National Park Service to preserve "one of the finest marine gardens in the Caribbean Sea."

1948
Buck Island is established as a "park" by the government of the Virgin Islands.

2001
President William Clinton enlarges the boundaries of Buck Island Reef National Monument to 19,015 acres.

1803
The slave ship General Abercrombie sinks close to the island, and all 339 slaves on board are saved.

1950
Goats are expelled from the Island. The island's native species of trees and vegetation begin to return.

Presidential Proclamation 3443 Establishing Buck Island Reef National Monument in the Virgin Islands of the United States by President John F. Kennedy

DECEMBER 28, 1961
by the President of the United States of America
A Proclamation

Whereas Buck Island, situated off the northeast coast of St Croix Island in the Virgin Islands of the United States, was included in the public, government, or crown lands ceded to the United States by Denmark under the convention entered into August 4, 1916, and proclaimed by the President January 25, 1917 (39 Stat. 1706); and

Whereas all property thus acquired by the United States from Denmark, not reserved by the United States for public purposes prior to June 22, 1937, was placed under the control of the Government of the Virgin Islands by the act of June 22, 1936, 49 Stat. 1807 (48 U.S.C. 1405-1405c), with the legal title remaining in the United States; and

Whereas Buck Island was not reserved by the United States for public purposes prior to June 22, 1937, but has been owned by the United States continuously since the convention with Denmark in 1916; and

Whereas Buck Island and its adjoining shoals, rocks, and under-sea coral reef formations possess one of the finest marine gardens in the Caribbean Sea; and

Whereas these lands and their related features are of great scientific interest and educational value to students of the sea and to the public; and

Whereas this unique natural area and the rare marine life which are dependent upon it are subject to constant threat of commercial exploitation and destruction; and

Whereas the Advisory Board on National Parks, Historical Sites, Buildings and Monuments, established pursuant to the act of August 21, 1935, 49 Stat. 666 (16 U.S.C. 463) impressed by the caliber and scientific importance of the coral reefs of Buck Island, has urged their prompt protection to prevent further despoliation; and

Whereas the Governor of the Virgin Islands, under the authority vested in him by the legislative assembly of the Virgin Islands by an act approved December 1961, has relinquished to the United States, for the purposes of facilitating the establishment and administration of a national monument for the protection of the above-mentioned areas and objects of historical and scientific interest, such control as is vested in the Government of the Virgin Islands by the said act of Congress dated June 22, 1936, over the area hereinafter described; subject, however, to the condition that the United States, including any agency or instrumentality thereof, shall not adopt or attempt to enforce any rule, regulation or requirement limiting, restricting or reducing the existing fishing (including the landing of boats and the laying of fishpots outside of the marine garden), bathing or recreational privileges by inhabitants of the Virgin Islands, and shall not charge any fees for admission to the area.

Whereas it is in the public interest to preserve this area of outstanding scientific, aesthetic, and educational importance for the benefit and enjoyment of the people:

Now, Therefore, I, John F. Kennedy, President of the United States of America, under and by virtue of the authority vested in me by section 2 of the act of June 8, 1906, 34 Stat. 225 (16 U.S.C. 431) do proclaim that, subject to valid existing rights, there is hereby reserved and set apart, as the Buck Island Reef National Monument, the area embraced within lines drawn between the coordinates of latitude and longitude recited as follows:

Beginning at latitude 17° 47′ 58″ N., longitude 64° 38′ 16″ W.; thence approximately 10,450 feet to latitude 17° 47′ 30″ N., longitude 64° 36′ 32″ W.; thence approximately 1,500 feet to latitude 17° 47′ 15″ N., longitude 64° 36′ 32″ W.; thence approximately 4,500 feet to latitude 17° 47′ 00″ N., longitude 64° 37′ 16″ W.; thence approximately 8,600 feet to latitude 17° 47′ 35″ N., longitude 64° 38′ 37″ W.; and thence approximately 3,075 feet to latitude 17° 47′ 58″ N., longitude 64° 38′ 16″ W., the place of beginning, embracing an area of approximately 850 acres.

WARNING is expressly given to all unauthorized persons not to appropriate, injure, destroy, deface, or remove any feature of this monument and not to locate or settle upon any of the lands reserved for the monument by this proclamation.

The Secretary of the Interior shall have the supervision, management, and control of this monument as provided in the act of Congress entitled "An act to establish a National Park Service, and for other purposes," approved August 25, 1916, 39 Stat. 535 (16 U.S.C. 1-3), and all acts supplementary thereto and amendatory thereof: Provided, that neither the Department of the Interior, nor any other agency or instrumentality of the United States, shall adopt or attempt to enforce any rule, regulation, or requirement limiting, restricting or reducing the existing fishing (including the landing of boats and the laying of fishpots outside of the marine garden), bathing or recreational privileges by inhabitants of the Virgin Islands, or charge any fees for admission to the area.

In Witness Whereof, I have hereunto set my hand and caused the Seal of the United States of America to be affixed.

DONE at the city of Washington this twenty-eighth day of December in the year of our Lord nineteen hundred and sixty-one, and of the Independence of the United States of America the one hundred and eighty-sixth.

John F. Kennedy

ON THE LAND

Buck Island is classified as a tropical dry forest and has been steadily returning to its original natural ecology since becoming fully protected in 1961. The island's vegetation includes Tamarind, Pigeon-Berry, Sandpaper, Frangipani, and Gum-Bo-Limbo trees, along with Organ-Pipe cactus. There are a few poisonous plants on the island that you should be aware of. The Manchineel tree can burn your skin if you touch its leaves, bark, or green apple fruit. And a plant called Christmas bush --which resembles holly—can cause a very uncomfortable rash.

The island serves as a habitat and nesting grounds for a variety of rare and protected species. The St. Croix Ground Lizard has been listed as endangered since 1977, and has been reintroduced on Buck Island. The brown pelican, which was on the endangered list from 1970-2009 due to the effects of over hunting and the pesticide DDT, has made a great comeback on the Monument. Recent monitoring indicates that a population of over 100 brown pelicans now live and hunt within the Monument's boundaries. And with respect to endangered vegetation, you can find the beautiful Sandy Point Orchid growing alongside cactus on the dry slopes of the island.

Buck Island beaches also serve as nesting grounds for 4 types of sea turtles -- Green, Leatherback, Loggerhead, and Hawksbill. The Hawksbill nesting story is particularly compelling. Most of the Hawksbill turtles that migrate to the Monument to nest are from the region around Nicaragua and Belize. Female Hawksbill mate every 2-3 years, and will build up to three separate nests, each containing 100 -150 eggs. The eggs take around 60 days to hatch, and the majority of the young turtles will be consumed by predators before even making it to the sea. In fact, it is estimated that the odds of an egg producing an adult Hawksbill turtle are only one in a thousand.

The National Park Service constantly monitors and collects data on all life forms that live within the Monument's boundaries.

REEF ECOLOGY

Coral reefs are living entities. They are constructed by thousands of animals called stony corals. Stony corals are comprised of polyps, which are very small organisms that range in size from 1 – 3 mm. As a polyp lives and dies, it leaves its skeleton behind where other polyps attach themselves and then follow the same life cycle. Over time a coral reef is built up by layer after layer of polyp skeletons that are fused together by algae and the force of underwater currents. Over the course of a year, corals can grow up to a half inch in size.

One of the most important facts that we can tell you about coral reefs is this: While coral reefs comprise less than 1% of the ocean's underwater terrain, they support and provide a habitat for 25% of all marine species. And while there are approximately 4,000 species of fish, there are over two million species of marine life that have been documented.

Although hard corals may appear to be sturdy and rock-hard, nothing could be further from the truth. The fact is that they are extremely fragile. The slightest touch by a careless snorkeler's fin, hand, or underwater camera can cause irreversible damage to coral, leaving it susceptible to disease and bleaching. The temperature and cleanliness of water -- along with its content of oxygen – can also affect the growth and health of coral polyps.

Soft corals exist in many forms on reefs. Common ones you may see on Buck's reef are sea fans, sea whips, and corky sea fingers. Soft corals may look like plants, but they too are comprised of living animals. They just don't have the rigid calcium exoskeletons that hard corals possess. But like hard corals, they are extremely fragile.

Coral reefs are complex, delicate environments that rely on a variety of interdependent relationships between life forms – hard and soft corals, fish, turtles, algae, sponges, and worms all playing important functions in the health and life of the reef.

Finally, coral reefs provide tremendous value to humanity. Reefs filter water, trap sediments, and protect the coastline from storms, waves, and floods. They provide tourism and recreation opportunities, and are great sources of food and medicine.

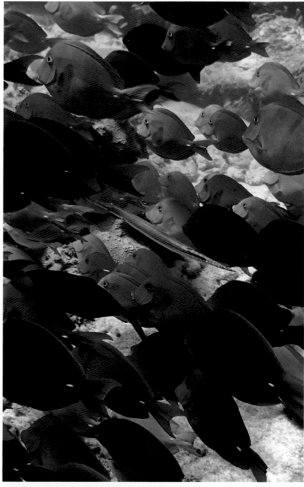

GETTING TO BUCK ISLAND

Concessionaires who conduct tours of Buck Island are sanctioned and licensed by the National Park Service. Currently, there are five privately owned tour companies that are official Park Service concessionaires. They offer either half day or full day trips, and usually provide drinking water and snorkeling gear. Before taking you to the underwater snorkeling trail, most outfitters will let you spend some time on beautiful Turtle Beach. Check out their web sites to choose a tour that fits your individual interests.

Authorized National Park Service concessionaires include:

BIG BEARD'S ADVENTURE TOURS
340-773-4482
www.bigbeards.com

Big Beard has been boating out to Buck Island for some 30 years now. His store is located right off the Christiansted Boardwalk on Queen Cross Street. Big Beard himself is a licensed St Croix minister, and has performed hundreds of weddings on his boats and in other tropical environments. Visit his website to choose from a variety of Buck Island tours.

CARIBBEAN SEA ADVENTURES
340-773-2628
www.caribbeanseaadventures.com

Captain Miles has been sailing the waters around Buck Island for over 40 years – since the age of 5! His company Caribbean Sea Adventures is located right on the Christiansted Boardwalk, and offers a variety of different Buck Island tours, accommodating groups from 2 to 150 people.

LLEWELLYN'S CHARTERS
340-773-9027
http://llewellynwesterman.com

Captain Llewellyn has over 50 years experience sailing the waters around Buck Island. His boat departs from Teague Bay, and he entertains his guests with his beautiful voice, singing songs of sailing and the Caribbean. His excursions to Buck are up close and intimate– usually taking 6 people at a time on his 37' custom built Trimarra.

JOLLY ROGER
340-513-2508
www.jollyrogervi.com

Captain Mike Klein will take you to Buck Island on his 42' sailing catamaran. Both half day and full day tours are offered, and his boats depart from the Christiansted Boardwalk right in front of "the mill"

TERORO II AND DRAGONFLY BUCK ISLAND CHARTERS
340-718-3161 *EMAIL – teroro@msn.com*

Captain Heinz and Carl are a father/son team who have been sailing for over 30 years. Their boats depart Green Cay Marina, and they accommodate groups ranging from 6 to 23 people.

Regulations

Because everything on the land and in the water is protected, there are a number of regulations you must follow when you visit Buck Island Reef National Monument. A good general rule of thumb to follow is to leave nothing behind on your visit, and take nothing else out with you except your memories, photographs, and trash. Be aware of the following rules:

- The Park is open from sunrise until sunset.
- Camping is not allowed on the island.
- No fishing, or possession of fishing equipment is allowed.
- Pets are prohibited.
- No feeding of fish or wildlife.
- No harvesting of any sort, plants, shells, rocks, and so on.
- Do not touch anything underwater.
- Do not stand on the reefs.
- No digging on the beaches of any kind.
- Beach umbrellas and volleyball nets are prohibited.
- No jet skiing or water skiing.
- Overnight anchoring permits must be applied for at the National Park Service office in Christiansted.
- A special use permit is required for groups over 20 people.

For a complete list of current regulations and permit applications, please visit the NPS website section on planning your visit: http://www.nps.gov/buis/planyourvisit/index.htm

SNORKELING BUCK ISLAND REEF

Buck Island's 10,000 year old barrier reef makes an arc around two thirds of the island, and forms a lagoon that lies between the shore and open seas. The snorkeling trail is located in this lagoon area off the southeastern tip of the island. The trail has underwater markers that explain the ecological features of the reef, and help guide you through it.

Concessionaires who bring you out to the snorkeling trail will first give you a guided tour through it before turning you loose to snorkeling around the area on your own. The maximum water depth here is around 12 feet, and you will be required to wear a supplied snorkeling vest. You will be exposed to a wide variety of corals during your snorkel, including huge specimens of brain coral and protected elkhorn coral. Snorkeling this part of the reef is usually a sea life extravaganza. You will have a good chance of seeing populations of reef fish of every color and description, along with squid, rays, and barracudas.

When you snorkel Buck Island reef, you will receive an education about the forces that effect the health and life of a reef. You will observe the leftover damage from 1989's Hurricane Hugo that destroyed 80% of Buck's reef. You will see examples of coral bleaching which is caused by rising ocean temperatures and disease. And if you are especially observant, you may spot a Lionfish. In the 1990's, Lionfish were introduced into the region by accident. Because they have a huge appetite for native fish populations and no known predators, they are threatening to upset the natural balance of area reef ecosystems.

Elkhorn Coral

Corky Sea Fingers

Sun Anenome

Spiny Sea Fan

Sea Fan

Lettuce Coral

Eliptical Star Coral

Maze Coral

Branching Vase Sponge

Blade Fire Coral

Branching Finger Coral

Scattered Pore Sponge

Staghorn Coral

Brain Coral

Yellow Ball Sponge

Long Spined Sea Urchin

Trumpet Fish

Queen Angel Fish

Scrawled Filefish

Puddingwife

Grey Angel Fish

Spotted Moray Eel

Blue Headed Wrasse

Yellow Goatfish

Pork Fish

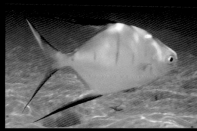

School Master

Palometa Jack

Yellow Tail Damsel Fish

FISH AND CORAL

Peacock Flounder

Reef Squid

Blue Striped Grunt Fish

Damsel Fish

Longfin Damselfish

Southern Ray

Trunk Fish

Four Eye Butterflyfish

Sergeant Major

Parrot Fish

Tang - Juvenile

French Grunt Fish

Blue Parrot Fish

Hound Fish

Yellowfin Mojarra

Barred Hamlet

Sheepshead Porgy

Damsel Fish

Stoplight Parrot Fish

Barracuda-Intermediate

Long Spine Squirrelfish

Red Hind Fish

Banded Butterfly Fish

Hawksbill Turtle

Yellow Head Wrasse

Blackbar Soldier Fish

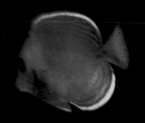

Blue Tang Fish Juvenile

FISH AND CORAL

Care for us by respecting our home, the reef where we live

The minute you step into the ocean, you become the house guest of a million different life forms. So be a great house guest:

Don't jump on the couch and don't steal the fine china! *(Translation: Don't stand on the reef and don't take coral and shells out of the ocean with you).*

Please support the following USVI environmental organizations who are working hard to protect, preserve, and grow the reefs. Visit their websites for updates on the invasive lionfish, the effects of suntan lotion ingredient oxybenzene on coral, and discover what you can do to support their efforts.

SEA - St. Croix Environmental Association
   www.stxenvironmental.org

REEF JAM - *www.reefjam.com*

VINE - Virgin Islands Network of Environmental Educators
   http://usvine.wordpress.com

THE NATURE CONSERVANCY - *www.nature.org*

EAST - Environmental Association of St. Thomas/St.John
   www.eastvi.org

FRIENDS OF VIRGIN ISLANDS NATIONAL PARK
   www.friendsvinp.org